The following contains two cookbooks in one. They both are dealing with cooking sensibly and economically, based on lessons learned from The Great Depression.

* * * *

COOKBOOK FOR HARD TIMES

Cooking Poor, but Healthy

* * *

Dedicated to my husband, Bill, who has always believed in me.

* * *

.

This is written by the daughter of parents who grew up in The Great Depression.

I have been cooking and baking all of my life. But I will admit it is not my career, so these are just my recipes which I have used down the years. So I present this cookbook, not as a perfect tool, nor an expert one, but just with the full intent that I hope people will find it helpful and enjoyable.

MY OLD STOVE

These are beginning lessons in cooking for difficult times. As the family budget gets tighter and times get harder, it is a good thing if someone in the home knows something about cooking. Unfortunately, this is becoming a dying art which I think should be brought back.

This book explains some basic principles which help a budget stretch. It includes a **Magic Grocery List** which helps the food be prepared more economically and makes it last longer in a budget which has to last two weeks, sometimes even a month.

There is a chapter on making bread. It has always been listed as one of the basic food groups in any diet. It is a staple, meaning one of the things most people want to have every day.

Basic meat recipes. This is something which can save money because it will help people prepare their own food sometimes, and save an eating out expense for that day, and it can provide satisfaction to the entire family, because it is a gift to the family when a
special meal is served to them prepared with love and good taste.

Homemade desserts. Snacks (that bad word to a diet), really might not be snacks at all. They could be a small meal. Some people have tea time. Either way, if the body is not satisfied, it will crave something, usually sweets. Everything in moderation, I believe. So why not make some cookies, muffins (light on the sugar), or a tea cake.

Gravies and Sauces have always been a part of meals, whether it is in spaghetti, or turkey and gravy. This is a talent and has to be mastered. If not, it is one of the main catastrophes of cooking a meal!

Soups There are so many ways to fix a delicious soup, and some of them are relatively easy. It is not only a quick meal, but also a healthy one to serve to someone who is feeling ill. A good soup can be strengthening to the body!

How to Cook Breakfast. Many times I have wished there was a how-to book for some obvious things, seemingly simple things, which it turned out, were very difficult for me to learn. So I decided to start with the basics of many people's idea of breakfast, one ingredient at a time. And that is what is in this book.

The Rest of the Pie. I was raised basically country. We have a lot of ways of saying things, which sometimes not everyone understands. We always back dozens of pies for holidays and at the end of this large family meal, invariably someone asks, "Now what do we do with the rest of the pie? Usually someone says, "I would like to have that, so we get out the plastic container for this, and send it home with them. I have heard many people say, "Oh, I don't eat leftovers!" As for me, I say, "Why on earth not?" We used to fight over the rest of the pie, especially if it was a favorite like homemade chocolate pie.

A Survival Kit for Hard Times. Actually I never thought I would be writing such a thing, but here it is. If times are tough and getting tougher, it might be a good thing to have there among the other cookbooks in the kitchen.

* * *

WHAT WAS THE GREAT DEPRESSION

And why do people still fear it today?

SOMETIMES THE SIMPLEST LIFE CAN BE THE BEST. TO
LIVE ECONOMICALLY, SIMPLIFY EVERYTHING, EVEN
PREPARING A MEAL

Chapter 1: The Magic Grocery Store List

Cooking poor is hard to do, but many people in today's economy have to learn to adjust their food budget. This means buying more economically at the grocery store, and also trying to feed hungry people on less money. Also you want everyone to stay healthy!

My name is Anna Patterson and I have been cooking all of my life. I was taught to cook by people who were a part of the people heavily influenced by their own part in the hardship which was The Great Depression.

With worldwide economic woes, it is very likely that the world could fall into similar crisis. The Great Depression was an economic problem of catastrophic proportions. It began in 1929 and by 1931 it had become a problem, in fact, a World Depression and was all over the world. When this economic decline ended is in debate, although this was seen as the early 1940's. That depression began with the fall of stock prices, and then a drop in personal income and a severe rise in unemployment.

Unfortunately, in the present day, these are the same growing problems.
I personally believe in being prepared, so I thought I would share some of the ways of cooking I was taught by people who did survive The Great Depression.

Because of this, I developed my own cheap cooking recipes. It was thrifty management practices in the kitchen, basically cooking cheaply, that kept families from starving to death during very hard times. So why not pass these old ways onto others.
It is a reassuring thing to an entire family when they have something satisfying to eat and can say, "And we are saving money on our food budget!"

What I remember about the Good Old Days is that they weren't always so good. Sometimes it seemed it was just plain hard living. I remember many people would make jokes about how old people would talk about how far they had to walk to school in the snow. I know I heard many stories of how hard people had it during The Great Depression.

People would often tell me, "Well, you wouldn't know what it was like, because we starved."

Of all the things which haunt the memories of those people who actually lived during these terrible times, there was a common thread:

!. Starving
2. Temporary or for long periods, homelessness
3. Trying to find work and keep it
4. Trying to pay for basic clothes and things like that.

So again, knowing how to buy food which would save money, is crucial.

Sometimes the old fashioned ways are best

So in hoping that things get better, but just in case they don't for a while, I decided to help people cook the old fashion penny pinching ways.

Going to the grocery store can kill a tight budget. So I have some advice. Never go there hungry, you will spend more. Also, never go there without a list. You will spend too much money. And last, but not least, stick to the list. These are still basics, but every person who does the Grocery Shopping for a family or just for their own self individually, needs to develop a Magic Grocery List (sensible, not wasteful, and something they will want to eat).

* * *

The Magic Grocery List

1. Bread

2. Milk (prefer powdered milk)

3. Sack of potatoes red or white

4. Sack of onions

5. Can of tomato juice

6. Coffee, tea

7. Basic staples: self-rising flour; margarine; shortening or lard; jelly

8. Spices: salt, pepper, chili powder

9. Mustard, mayonnaise or salad dressing

10. Rice, macaroni

11. Beans, dry, any kind

12. Oats

13. Meat: whole chicken, hamburger, tuna, hot dogs, cheese

14. Canned corn, green beans, assorted vegetables

15. One food which is a treat for that month, pizza or something like that.

16. Fruit which is in season

I believe in this list, with slight variations such as including fruit when in season. This is just a starter list, and you will need to add favorite things and modify to suit family, but if you are pinching pennies, these are basic needs.

* * * * *

BEFORE YOU GO TO THE GROCERY STORE, THINK
ABOUT WHAT YOU WANT TO COOK, AND HOW YOU PLAN
TO DO SO

Chapter 2: Bread

Biscuits

Baking Powder biscuits: 425 oven for 10 minutes

Two cups flour, one teaspoon salt, four teaspoons baking powder, two tablespoons shortening, and three-fourths cup of milk.

Mix dry ingredients, sift twice, or just stir together with spoon many times. Work the shortening in with a knife or spoon. Add liquid. Drop by spoonfuls into baking pan which has been greased or muffin pan, greased.

Bake at 450 degrees for twelve to fifteen minutes. For variety, sprinkle with a teaspoon of cinnamon before stirring together with a teaspoon of sugar.

Always remember: Take care of the pennies and the dollars will take care of themselves.

My Personal views about bread, is it is always necessary in some form.

Some bread is just too expensive to make and it is cheaper to buy a loaf of bread, but then again, for a very tight budget the solution might be basic bread supplies:

FLOUR: plain flour for making yeast breads. Then you have to buy the yeast and follow directions. You also need some sugar, and milk.

Basic rolls are made with four cups of milk; two packages compressed yeast, four tablespoons of sugar, eight cups of four, one tablespoon of salt and one half cup unmelted shortening.

Always put the flour in a bowl only after making the yeast rise according to directions. Once it has risen, put flour in bowl, add salt, and then add the milk, shortening. Then the yeast, and cover and put a towel over this. Let rise for about an hour on kitchen shelf or table. When it rises, grease pan and shape with hands into round balls on pan. Bake at hot oven, about 425 until lightly brown on top.

* * * * *

Cornbread comes in mixes or as self rising. Bake at 400 degree oven for 20 minutes.

For biscuits and pancakes get self rising flour if you don't want to get baking powder.

Pancakes can be made by just putting two cups of self rising flour in bowl, add one half cup milk. Add one egg. Fry in pan with shortening melted and covering bottom of pan (about tablespoon shortening). Fry this and then turn it over when you see edges are firm and turning brown. Some people buy powdered sugar and when pancakes are done just powder them with the powdered sugar, but most of the time just put butter on them and syrup. If you run out of syrup, just use a little jelly on the finished pancakes.

MAKING DO WITH LITTLE

Surprise your family on the holidays by learning to bake dressing and things like that.

Dressing

Dressing can be made from left over cornbread which I freeze and save for this, or from bread, again the left over bread, such as any bread which I freeze.

Take the bread, chicken broth (about a quart at a time) until very moist, it is according to how much bread you have. Add onions, I like to add shredded carrots for texture and health reasons. I also add celery, chopped or flakes. Then add sage, you need to add this one tablespoon at a time. If you have a large bowl you are making into dressing, then one tablespoon will do it. For more, double the amount of sage. I taste a spoonful of mixture. Sometimes, if I have them, I add two chopped boiled eggs. Salt and pepper I leave to the people who are eating it since most of the people I know are on salt restricted diets.

* * *

Dumplings

Three cups of Self-Rising Flour. One and one-third milk. Two eggs for rich dumplings.

Chicken broth from boiled chicken. I leave the chicken in it in a roaster pan. When the chicken is basically done, I add spoonfuls of heaping dumplings, added on top of the cooked meat. Must cover with lid immediately, but if pan is too full, will spill over when dumplings rise, so leave a slit of lid open and even check on these and cook five minutes, and then five minutes more. Then take lid off and cook until dumplings are firm and cooked through. You can check this by taking one out into bowl and cutting it in half. If still raw inside, return to pan and keep cooking.

If you want to get fancy, sprinkle with parsley flakes when you serve the chicken and dumplings.

* * * * *

Chapter Three Quick Cooking

When I am really economizing, I start with oats or rice and toast for breakfast, and a soup or light casserole for lunch or sandwich

and then what all of my life I have heard called, "a nice dinner."
Nonetheless, I believe breakfast can be extremely important, and
have always preferred to fix a big breakfast at times.

SOUP WITHOUT MEAT

Six potatoes

Three or four tomatoes

Two bell peppers

Two onions and one spoon butter.

Cook until tender, then in a cup take two tablespoons flour, one third cup milk and blend and then add to soup to thicken.

FRENCH TOAST

Use sliced bread. One egg in bowl. Add dash cinnamon (one-fourth teaspoon until you learn to just add a dash of this or a dash of that like grandmothers did during The Great Depression. I remember asking my own grandmother how much of a spice to add and she would say, "Open the lid to the sprinkle side and just hold it over the bowl and shake it into it once. That is a dash of the spice."

If you don't want to try this, then open the space on the larger side and put a teaspoon into it and get it by the half teaspoon or less until you learn your spices more.

I put about one-fourth cup of milk in this.

Mix up all ingredients except bread. Put bread in and soak well on both sides. Fry this in grease like you would pancakes and when finished you add a little sugar if you have a sweet tooth or salt and pepper if you don't.

* * *

TUNA FISH SANDWICH

Tuna, mayonnaise, onion, one boiled egg. Mix well and put between two pieces of bread. Some people like to toast the bread first.

* * *

TACOS

Taco shells

Lettuce chopped fine. Onions chopped fine. Cheese shredded.

Hamburger cooked with a taco mix or with homemade mix below.

HOMEMADE MIX FOR TACOS

To cooked and drained hamburger, add three cups tomato juice, one tablespoon chili powder, one teaspoon cumin. Simmer (that means a low fire, but still bubbling, about five minutes.

To make tacos, first take shell, add meat mixture, and then top with the dry stuff. You are done.

* * *

BEANS AND CORNBREAD

One of the best things you can have in a kitchen is a good and safe crock pot. Take pinto beans, rinse. Put these in crock pot. I usually put about three cups of beans in it and cover them with water. I add an onion sliced for flavor and sometimes add mustard like you buy to put on a hot dog. I only add one tablespoon of the mustard. If you want the beans real flavorful add my secret ingredient (brown sugar only a half cup with molasses about one tablespoon).

Cook all night.

If you are a meat person, add ham hocks to this, about four of these.

SALMON CROUQUETTES

Take one or two cans of salmon and don't drain, but pick out bones. Some remove skin, I don't. Crumble this up in a bowl with at least two whole crackers, or four small crackers. Add two eggs, one tablespoon of flour per can of salmon and the mix thoroughly and drop by spoonfuls into melted shortening in a frying pan and brown and turn. You can substitute tuna for this instead of salmon and I have also done this with mackerel.

* * *

Chapter 4 Basic Meat Recipes

NOTHING IS MORE BASIC THAN HAMBURGER

When times are hard, then people have to live with less and the people who survived The Great Depression learned to accept living in a simple way.

STARTING WITH A CHICKEN IN THE POT

I can personally remember going out to the chicken house and gathering chickens eggs. I also remember cooking a fresh plucked chicken. But I am modernized as the next person, so I buy a whole chicken, wash it and then put it in a pot and boil it in water on about a medium flame until the chicken falls off the bone. I add water if I need to.

Boiling meat is simple to fix. You can do this with a roast beef or roast pork

And there is always the obvious: How to cook hamburger!

HAMBURGERS

Frying hamburgers is a simple task and favorite to many. IF using regular hamburger meat, just shape into patties and fry in ungreased skillet on a fairly mild flame or heat until you can see it browning all along edges. Flip it over and cook the other side. If you use ground chuck, I add a little shortening because otherwise it will stick on the skillet and some of the meat is wasted.

You can make an onion burger if you chop onions and add them to the cooking hamburgers just shortly before the hamburgers are done. I turn the heat off and melt the cheese while the meat is still in the pan.

MEATBALLS

In a bowl mix meat, about two pounds, bread crumbs made from toasting two pieces of bread, two eggs, and onions if you desire. Shape into meatballs and brown in skillet. Stir while cooking. When done, drain. These can be used by themselves or with tomato sauce or spaghetti sauce, and spaghetti.

MEATLOAF

Mix your meat, about four pounds of hamburger with three pieces of bread not toasted, crumbled, three eggs, one onion chopped, and shape into a loaf and put in oven. On top of this, pour tomato catsup and smooth out with knife. May cover with aluminum foil and bake.

SWISS STEAK

Take a steak or ground chuck and cook in grease after flouring meat. Cook completely and then add green pepper sliced or diced and onion, and tomatoes, whole in can or sliced fresh. Cook total mixture about ten minutes. This can be served with microwave baked potato. Add sour cream out of the container to potato.

HOMEMADE INDOOR BARBECUE.

Roast pork or beef cooked and chopped up. Add any barbecue sauce and half cup of water and mix thoroughly while meat is hot, and put on bread or buns.

* * * * *

Chapter 5. Homemade Desserts

Basic cookie baking. Dropped cookies bake at 350 to 400 for about 10 minutes

Cobblers

Cake 375 degrees for about 25 minutes.

Pastry for cobblers

Three cups flour, one cup shortening, one teaspoon salt and half cup of water. If dough is too dry add a little more water until dough is able to be shaped with hands, but still a little sticky. Mix and then flour wax paper, and press out dough and cut into strips with knife, then place in pan which has been greased and lightly floured.

Cobblers

Always take the pastry and just roll out into flat sheet. Cut this into strips and layer this with any canned fruit with a cup of sugar added. Use all juice in large can, and you can double this if you want. I add cinnamon or nutmeg to cobblers.

If you want to make from fresh fruit, I would slice and dice apples and cook them until fairly soft and then make the cobbler out of this.

* * * * *

Chapter 6: Gravy and Sauces

It seems to me, personally, that Holiday dinners are just loaded with special sauces and gravies. That is why we groan about the calories, but I love the Holidays, so I include recipes which will help a family save money by their buying and cooking the meal.

The basic sauces for a good cook:

HOMEMADE GRAVY

I make gravy out of the grease left by sausage or some meat like that. I save leftover grease in a bowl in the icebox. Sometimes I fry pork chops and use the left over grease. I add a tablespoon of flour at a time and stir until it mixed thoroughly. Gather by stirring with a spoon into the middle of a pan and let it then float out back over the pan. It should do this or it is too thick and you will have to add more milk or even water if you don't have any king of milk at all. Lower heat because it will boil over when it really starts bubbling. Brown flour in grease lightly and then add liquid, about two cups of milk, cream, or even water. Boil and stir at times until thick. If you add too much liquid and it is thin, cook longer so some of this will cook out of it. Salt and pepper as you choose.

WHITE SAUCE

Take two tablespoons of butter or margarine, and melt on slow heat. Add two tablespoons of four and one cup of milk and stir until thick.

MEAT STOCK GRAVY

For this you need to reserve the broth which comes after you roast any meat. I let this cool and save in a jar sometimes or a pan other times. Use within a few days. Take the stock and pour into a pan and start heating this. This is meat stock gravy, chicken or beef. The take a cup and add three tablespoons of flour, one half cup water or milk. Stir the cup mixture well. Then slowly add it to the meat broth and mix well. Cook on low heat, but boiling until thickened.

* * *

The Holiday Grocery Shopping List

1. Cranberries in bag. Cook according to directions.

2. Carrots and green beans. Open can, heat and add butter while these are still hot.

3. Some type of CASSEROLE

Yams out of can, with miniature marshmallows for example, or corn with green peppers diced and one red bell pepper for color.

4. Turkey whole baked in oven according to directions. Or buy a turkey pan, wash turkey and put this in pan, cover with foil tight after rubbing turkey with butter or margarine.

Cook until completely done. Legs will pull from rest of turkey easily when done. If any bleeding occurs, it's not done.

Thaw out turkey in advance according to package instructions.

* * * * *

Chapter 7: Soups

Anyone who has ever been through Hard Times personally knows that the first rule is just accept you can live more modestly and do better and be happier.

CHICKEN SOUP

Cut up chicken, water and cook until tender and done. Add can mixed vegetables, two if you are adding this to large chicken. Add tomato juice if desired. Add rice or macaroni if you wish.

BEEF VEGETABLE

To make quick soup, buy two cans mixed vegetable soup, use some tomato juice and reserve the rest for drinking or making other things. Add leftover beef, chopped well, and heat and eat.

POTATO SOUP

Cook potatoes, about six peeled and cubed. When soft, add chopped onions, one tablespoon celery flakes. Add teaspoon oregano. In a small skillet make a thickening sauce with one half cup shortening, melt this, then add a tablespoon flour and mix well heating slightly, then add cup of milk. Bring this to a boil and then turn off. When cooled enough to lift with pot holder, then add it to your potato soup which is simmering. Cook fifteen minutes and then it is ready to serve. People can add their own salt and pepper as desired.

END OF THE MONTH SOUP

Never say you can't make homemade soup. I put left over green beans, carrots, and potatoes in a bowl and when I want to make soup, I get this out, some tomato juice, left over roast of any kind, or left over chicken, boned thoroughly or even left over, but still fresh fish and I mix this together. I like to add to this an onion soup mix and macaroni. That is basically it.

POTATO SALAD

Cooked diced potatoes, cooled

Mustard out of bottle, one tablespoon.

Mayonnaise or salad dressing one cup

Boiled and diced three eggs

Celery, fresh and diced if desired

Add diced onion if desired

Mix and chill.

* * * * *

Chapter 8: How to Cook Breakfast

Shown are cheese eggs with sausage

HOW TO COOK AN EGG

I have never assumed everyone knows everything, so basics first. Crack an egg in a bowl. I have seen beginners crack an egg on the counter and they end up dripping it all of the way to the floor. I have seen people crack against the hot pan where they burn themselves and immediately some of the egg runs under the skillet and started smoking the burner and the pan. And I have seen them actually make it into the pan only to bust the yellow and get egg shells into the food. Lets not do that!

FRIED EGG

Crack into a bowl and reserve.

Start about two tablespoons of shortening in a shallow pan on a moderate heat and then add egg. Cook on one side until firm and then turn over and cook other side. If you want yellow done cook until the yellow looks like a well done boiled egg yellow and then take this up.

A. SCRAMBLED EGG

Beat the egg (or if cooking for a family, beat the eggs. Add milk to this, and cook in melted butter or shortening. Pour it in and left it start firming up, stir often, when completely firm, take up and serve.

How to boil rice

Follow directions on the box. I know that seems too easy, but it works. Do the same with oats and pancakes.

* * * * *

Chapter 9: The Rest of the Pie

I have read many times; if we don't remember the lessons we learned from history, we are destined to repeat them. I believe the old fashioned ways are often best when times get tough.

STRETCHING THE MEAL

There is a name for it, quantity cooking. One way you can cook easily for a large group, is make a spaghetti dish. Also chili and crackers might be a good idea. But one of the most versatile vegetables on earth is the potato, so if you really want to be able to make your budget work, learn different ways to use potatoes. Here are just a few:

CHICKEN POT PIE

Start with a baked chicken, bones removed, and six large potatoes, one can of English peas and one can of sliced carrots. Mix all of this with broth of chicken about three cups. I take a can of biscuits and top the meat pie I have made and put in oven until biscuit top is nice and brown.

CREAMED POTATOES

Take at least four potatoes, possibly to six and cook in stew pan with water just to cover. If you put a lid on this, leave a crack open for steam to escape. Cook until tender when you check with fork. Drain liquid and reserve. Then add a tablespoon of butter, a half cup of milk and mix even with a fork or mixer until creamy. If it needs more milk, add, but put butter on table if people want to add more.

HOMEMADE FRENCH FRIES

If you want to make French Fries, it is all on how you cut them. Start by peeling the potatoes. Then slice them into wedges. Then take a wedge and either third or fourth it. This should give you the French Fried style people are used to seeing. Then heat shortening, you need about three cups and drop a few cups of these French Fries at a time. They should brown properly and you can stir about once, not too much. Take up and drain. Be sure they are soft on inside or they are not done. If you try to fry them too hot, they will brown too quickly on outside and not cook on inside. If you find you have done this, you could put them in the microwave for about five minutes to tenderize the inside without burning to a crisp the outside.

Remember! Even in the kitchen, an obvious failed attempt can be salvaged.

MICROWAVED BAKED POTATOES

I remember when I bought my first microwave, and I am still learning neat things about it. One of these is how to bake one potato in about five minutes. I just put the potato in there. Heat it to five minutes. Check to see if a fork will go through it, and if it does, I take it out. If it doesn't, I try a few more minutes. If making about six or eight potatoes for a quick meal with guests, I go for about ten or fifteen minutes. Sometimes slightly longer. It is according to the size of the potato and the size of the microwave also.

* * *

MAKING HOMEMADE FRUIT JUICES

Take Apples, peaches, grapes and wash and then cut out stem and seeds of large fruits with these and just stem of small fruits. Cover with cold water and cook on low to medium heat at slow boil. Stir at times and when fruit falls apart, turn off and remove from heat. When cool remove seeds and grind up fruit in food processor. Use a little of juice if you need to grind this up good this way, but if you use too much it will pour out of food processor. When it is a fine pulp, then put in a pitcher with remaining juice and add water, about a quart or two until it is a thin mix resembling any liquid fruit drink. Sweeten with a cup of sugar or artificial sweetener and let it set in ice box preferable all night before drinking.

Tomato juice is the same only I add a teaspoon of Tabasco sauce to mine.

APPLESAUCE

Pare with a stainless steel knife and core and then slice apples. Add one and one-half cups water to each quart of sliced apples.

Cover and cook to a mush. 35 minutes for a peck.

Press through sieve or mash in food processor. Sweeten to taste.

VEGETABLES AS A MUST

The cheap help for the cook

CABBAGE

Wash and discard those mushy and browned parts. Cut in about fourths and then slice. Cover with water and cook. Add a piece of raw bacon or to if you want for seasoning and salt and pepper.

FRIED GREEN TOMATOES

About eight green tomatoes, small. Slice these real thin and dip in an egg mixed with a fork with half cup milk. Fry in shortening until brown and take out and drain some before serving.

FRIED OKRA

Always wash this and take top off and small tip off. Slice into pieces, not lengthwise, but into as many slices as you can, about six to a pod. Dip these into cornmeal and then fry until brown.

EGG PLANT.

Do this the same as the Okra, only use cracker crumbs to dip it into instead of cornmeal.

POTATOES

A. Cream potatoes -- Peel potatoes, cover with water, cook until tender. Pour off water after cools down some and reserve the water to use in gravy if you want to. Take the potatoes and mash with a fork thoroughly or a mixer. Add butter, milk, salt and pepper.

B. Fried potatoes -- Microwave potatoes in peeling. About five or ten minutes for three. Check by trying to stick a fork into it. If you can it is done. Wait until it cooks slightly and wash off and then peel and slice as French fries. Drain thoroughly and then drop in hot grease and fry until brown and then take out and drain and serve.

* * * * *

Chapter 10: A Survival Kit for Hard Times

Throughout the history of the World, people have looked to their leaders to bring them out of the economic hardships they are enduring. Time after time, history has repeated itself on this.

The harsher the time and distress, the more the people seek relief through the leaders of that period. But it seems to me, the true survival of these tough times will much depend upon the survival skills of the people facing these acute problems.

Living through Hard Times, I have found time again, people have told me, depends upon their own faith, strong will, and resourcefulness. As people try to live on less, or at least spend less, it helps to start in the kitchen, which can be the most extravagant spending place of any family. So I hope this little cookbook will be a help to the people who read it.

With a loss of economic opportunity, it does take resourcefulness and a willingness to go back to the old ways to survive.

THE END

######

Book Two

BACK TO BASICS: COOKING FOR THE GREAT DEPRESSION

Cookbook for people who have to pinch pennies

The Great Depression, along about 1929, the global world had problems which escalated into something called by this name. It was such a huge economic crisis that the world will never forget it.

Quite simply, many people suffered in severe economic times. This means for many homelessness, extreme starving, and a depressed life style which was caused by unemployment.

Many people feel the world as a whole is struggling with all of these issues today. These are tough times. Unemployment still stays at a level where many millions are unemployed.

There has been an increase in the number of people who through no fault of their own, have sunk down to the poverty level of living. The number of people going hungry without reassurance they can eat, that to, is climbing.

I hope that all of this and the other unstable economic factors don't continue to lead to another Great Depression, but I believe *it is better to be safe, than sorry.*

This cookbook is designed to help people who are scaling down their budget for any reason, and yet want to continue to adequately feed themselves and their family.

This book is written and shared with love. Hope it helps, and will be a benefit to people who cook out of necessity and love for those who they serve.

* * * *

YEAST BREADS

Most people the world over; continue to think bread one of the most important items on the family's menu.

Yeast bread is something which it is wise to learn to make.

It should be baked in a 375 degree oven.

1. Start with one cake compressed yeast
One tablespoon sugar
Two cups liquid (milk or water)

2. seven cups flour
One-half tablespoon salt
Two tablespoons melted shortening (or left over bacon grease)

3. Put the yeast in a bowl; add sugar and a little liquid. Cover and let rise about five minutes

4. Then add yeast to all liquid. Add flour little at a time until this is mixed into the liquid mixture. Sprinkle with the salt and continue to mix. Mix until all dough is holding together. Since you are adding flour a little at a time, when you have stiff dough, stop adding flour and use this to flour board or clean table or cabinet. Place your dough on a clean surface so you can knead it. Mash it down and repeat this about 12 times. If it sticks to surface, sprinkle with more flour. If you make it too dry, sprinkle a little lukewarm water on this. Dough needs to look fairly smooth, hold together well, and be able to be kneaded several times.

Then put in a bowl and cover with cloth, and let rise until double. This takes several hours.

Making bread like this takes time, and patience, but it is worth it.

After this take out and knead again about five minutes (mashing and turning over and mashing again.

After this, put dough in well greased bread pans and Bake.

* * *

GINGERBREAD UPSIDE DOWN CAKE

An oldie but a goodie

1. Get this together and wait until you mix flour mixture

One tablespoon margarine
One-fourth cup brown sugar
Four slices canned pineapple, drained.
One-third cup sugar
One teaspoon ginger,
One of cinnamon,
One-fourth teaspoon cloves
One egg, well beaten
One-half cup molasses
One-half cup water

2. Flour mixture:
Two cups self rising flour
Otherwise add tablespoon baking powder and one teaspoon salt

One-fourth cup shortening.

Sift flour, baking powder and salt together if you don't use self rising. Mix shortening into this with a fork. Mix well.

Melt margarine in an 8" x 8" x 2" cake pan. Sprinkle with brown sugar.

Cut pineapple slices in halves and arrange on top of sugar.

Measure the flour mix into mixing bowl.

Stir in the sugar and spices. Then egg, molasses and water. Add these gradually stirring until well blended. Pour this mixture over the fruit in the pans. Bake at 350 degrees. Cool before turning these

Oldies but goodies

No matter what occupations and interests we connect with in our life, cooking can be its own reward.

I have heard the expression its old, but it is still good. When economic times become rough, this is a good saying to remember!

* * *

Chapter 1: Saving the family budget

I guess I learned millions of old sayings when I was a child. Many are about the passage of time. Time does march on. When planning the month's budget, it is easy to hurry through the month without planning for the meals, and looking back regret the waste of much of the family's money due to waste of money.

I read once that time, every minute of it, is more valuable than gold.

An example of a lifetime meal plan and an old idea, but still good

For Breakfast: fruit, coffee or tea

Luncheon: cold meat, fish or eggs; salad, toast, fruit

Dinner: Meat, poultry, fish or eggs, green vegetables, dry toast, salad, fruit small coffee

A health tip: one hour before meal, drink a glass of water

Eat plain foods basically, not sauces, gravies, condiments

AVOID too much of these:

Salt, preservatives, starchy vegetables, sweetened fruit, sweet drinks of all kinds, confections and candies.

A practical diet, a modest diet, is a good game plan

* * *

There is no getting around it, the body has to have energy and this comes from food. When people face hard times, it becomes more and more difficult to supply this Life Saving Energy Source!

* * *

So healthy foods can include:

Figs, fruit juices, peaches, pears, plums

AND

Spinach or other greens, tomatoes, vegetables of all kinds

AND

Meats, soups, jelly and preserves

AND
Bread and desserts

Remember the thing about dieting and just plan eating is use common sense, eat for two; you will be the size of two!

The best diet is, eat what you need to, after that shut your mouth, and just don't eat it, I don't care what it is!

* * *

Always be on the lookout for kitchen utensils, at second hand shops, yard sales, on line, anywhere you might pick them up, and then keep them, and most of all, use them. Always clean them good with very hot, soapy water.

Old time Hint: You need to hold a match or tooth pick between your teeth while peeling onions, and the fumes won't make you cry.

* * *

WHAT CAN WE HAVE FOR A NICE DINNER?

Once upon a time menu, another oldie, but a good one:

Cream of Pea Soup
Baked Slice of Ham
Spinach
Lettuce salad with light dressing
One layer cake

* * *

BREAD TODAY

I have seen a time, when bread was made every day
Started before the light hit the skies, by a weary person
Working in the kitchen, against the rising of the sun,
Because bread had to be baked before the children
Walked to school, or the farm hands went out to chores.

40

HAULING HAY TODAY

Carrying a couple of biscuits in a sack on the tractor
Hope that will hold me, and keep me from passing out,
The field is big; the hay has to be brought in,
It's going to be a long, long hot day,
But I've got a sack of homemade biscuits,
I can do it. I've got to do it.

* * *

IT'S A POTLUCK BARN RAISING

Well everybody knew it was a job, hadn't they prepared for this day for months and the lumber and stuff was there

So they sat the tables up on one side and the women brought their food, some of the best cooks of that state,

And people worked like mad dogs, and the lumber went up,

Sometime that day, when this began to look like a barn, work stopped

And people came to the table and ate like they were starving, and they were.

By sundown, that barn was up there for everybody to see.

* * *

YOU WANT SOMETHING SWEET?

ANGEL CREAM PARFAIT

One cup sugar
One cup water
Two teaspoons orange extract
Two teaspoons strawberry extract

Two pints whipping cream

41

Stir in sugar and water and stir on low fire until sugar dissolves.

Simmer slowly and test small amount by dropping in cold water and it can roll into a ball.

Whip six egg whites stiff and pour six tablespoonfuls of the syrup into the whites, whipping constantly, stir hard, add extracts and when cold fold into cream.

Put in freezing pans and leave for four hours

* * *

Dear Friend:

Do you have a favorite recipe handed down for generations? Most families do. Along with the photos and other mementos of past days, nothing is more special than that recipe which becomes dearer as the years go by.

If you don't have such a thing, buy a notebook or note cards and start collecting these on your own. I have a chili recipe which has been on an internet web site for many years now. I like to think people are still making that simple chili recipe I created so long ago.

* * *

Cantaloupe, bananas, oranges, pears, what ever is in season that is the dessert or snack when on a budget. Anything else is just a delightful surprise dish!

HINT:

Serve bananas with ice-cream, a smaller amount of ice cream will then be needed.

Peaches can be eaten basically as is, or serve with cereal, ice-cream, or make pies and cobblers with them.

Pumpkin is versatile, cook like a potato and mash it, and serve as vegetable, or put it in a pie and serve pumpkin pie.

Strawberries can be eaten fresh, just cut stems off and wash them, or crush them and serve with a plain, not iced cake, and whipped cream. Some people make their own strawberry preserves. But since strawberry preserves take about nine or ten cups of sugar, preserves are usually cheaper to buy than to make, and of course it is a while lot easier.

* * *

Pineapple is another thing which has many recipes because it is an all time favorite!

* * *

Few people nowadays grow their own food, and even fewer do the canning of this food which used to be a way of life in an earlier time. Now it is so much simpler, but costs so much more too even buy the basic nutrition everyone has to have to survive.

* * * *

WHAT IS CALLED STAPLES

A grocery list for the week or for the month should have what is called staples. That means basic things which will help one make a good and satisfying meal.

My list of staples always includes:
Potatoes
Macaroni
Bread
Some type of fruit
Chicken or hamburger
Cereal
Milk
One dessert

Based on many things, a staple list has to fit the family's needs and the situation.

* * *

TALKING TO COOKS

I think if I got a room full of cooks together, each one would have a different way of cooking things, but they would all agree on one thing, the proof of whether or not a meal was good, is the plate which comes back to the kitchen. Was the food eaten or not? If not, no matter how expensive or nice a dish, it failed the taste test.

* * *

BAVARIAN CREAM

A very old recipe

Two tablespoons of Gelatin
One half cup of cold water
One can pineapple
One half cup sugar
One tablespoon lemon juice
One cup of whipped cream

Soak the gelatin in the cold water. Heat the pineapple, sugar and lemon juice. Beat the gelatin into the above ingredients, well and let cool. Beat in the cream and let completely cool.

* * *

Hint: There are a few items which are always worth the money you spend on them. With people having little time to cook, they also need to save time. I use a food processor to chop and grind food. I also have a blender for all sorts of things which I like to make, and I have an electric roaster oven that I can cook a whole turkey or chicken in.

Another thing which I think is helpful is to have old fashioned things in your kitchen, a rolling pin, a non electric can opener, a bottle opener, tea strainer, and things like that. I have collected many of these items from garage sales and second hand stores and you can also. These are just as helpful nowadays as I am sure they were in the past.

*　*　*

COST SAVING DRINK: TEA

In a saucepan, boil about one cup of water. Turn off when at full boil. Add four small tea bags or two large tea bags for pitcher of tea.

I use a plastic tea pitcher, so I put a lid on the finished tea and let it set for a while. Then I add water to the tea pitcher about two-thirds full, then the tea. You can add water to the tea bags and actually bring to a boil again to make another pitcher of tea.

I do this every time. My husband drinks sweetened tea, so I add a cup of sugar to his tea pitcher while it is hot and stir.

Then I put this in the ice box and serve it chilled and iced. I, on the other hand cannot use sugar, so I make the second batch mine and make it without sugar.

Many people drink tea totally unsweetened in any way, and this is how I like it.

*　*　*

Hint: For burns to the skin when something splashes on it by an accident, an egg white is good to spread over a fresh burn, and can usually take it away.

*　*　*

THE LOVE OF COOKING

I really believe that in this cookbook the main thing I hope to share is a joy for cooking. I can remember my very first experiences with cooking, and how I loved it when my grandmother would show me how to make chicken and dumplings.

My Mother saw that I enjoyed cooking and went out and bought me a complete set of encyclopedia's of cooking before I entered junior high school.

She would buy me the ingredients and she and my father liked to see what type of meal I would come up with.

I believe I cooked just about everything in these books for years and because of that I have a love of food from different countries as well as those I learned at my grandmother's. To this day, my cooking reflects many nationalities of good and healthy foods.

* * *

Some people save coupons, some people try to stock up groceries during sales.

* * * *

Chapter 2: Why not think about a good breakfast?

French toast: three eggs, dash milk, mix. Add a sprinkle of Cinnamon. Drop bread in this. Then fry until brown. Serve with syrup and butter.

* * *

PINEAPPLE MUFFINS

Two and one-half cups flour
Four tablespoons butter
One-half teaspoon salt
One-half cup Evaporated milk diluted with one-half cup water
Five teaspoons baking powder
Four tablespoons sugar
One egg
One can crushed pineapple.

Sift dry ingredients into a bowl. Combine melted butter, beaten egg and liquid. Mix wet and dry ingredients.
Pour into greased muffin tins.
Bake at about 400 for 20 minutes or until firm.

* * *

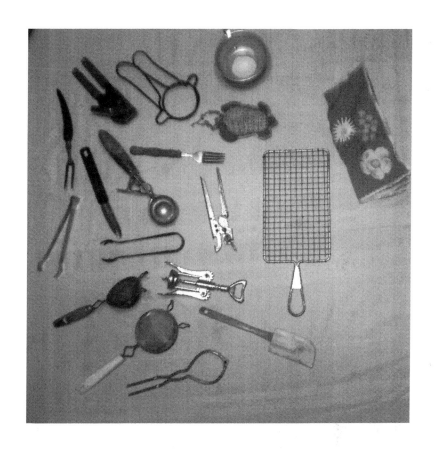

QUICK MUFFINS

Preheat oven at 400 degrees, 25 minutes

One fourth cup butter
One-fourth cup sugar
One egg
Two cups self -rising flour
One cup of milk
Mix butter and sugar together well. Add egg. Add flour and milk a little at a time.

Bake in greased small muffin pan. Might be wise to double recipe

* * *

CORN BREAD

Temperature 375 until brown on top, about 35 minutes

One cup boiling water
One-half cup yellow cornmeal
One-half teaspoon salt
One-half tablespoon butter
One cup milk
Two eggs
Add cornmeal to boiling water slowly and stir. Cook until thick. Remove and add salt and butter. Add milk, eggs.
Place in shallow greased baking pan and bake.

* * *

Hint:
For those who have not cooked much or at all, to cook sausage in a pan, either cook it slow enough so that it will make some grease and not stick, or add a little grease to pan before you make the sausage meat into patties. Then cook until brown on both sides.

* * *

BASIC SPICES FOR COOKING
Pepper black used in meat and vegetable dishes.
Garlic: This is a vegetable similar to onion, but with bulb divided into seconds known as cloves. This may be used in small amounts in flavoring meats, soups, sauces, salads and pickles.

* * *

WHAT DOES STEWING MEAN?
This is cooking in liquid below the boiling point.
Frying is cooking in fat.
Braising is browning in fat, then adding some liquid and simmering.

* * *

CEREAL AND BANANAS

Try enriching breakfast cereal, hot or cold, with milk or cream, sugar, and top this with sliced banana. This is an old favorite!

* * *

SOUTHERN CORNBREAD

Self rising flour, three cups; three tablespoons shortening, or half cup cooking oil. To this add 3.4 cup corn meal, 1.4 teaspoon salt

Two tablespoons sugar,

Two eggs, three/fourths cup of milk.

It needs to add more milk to make smoother like cake mix then do so.

Fill well-greased oven pan and bake at 400 for about 20 minutes, until well brown.

* * *

BREAKFAST SUGGESTIONS

1. Oatmeal, bacon, coffee, cream, muffins
2. Sausage patties, apple jelly or sauce, coffee cake, orange juice
3. fruit, canned or fresh; eggs any style, toast, coffee
4. Cereal out of a box, one piece French toast, coffee

* * * *

BISCUITS

Two cups Self-rising flour (so you want have to add baking powder and salt). Mix with three-fourths cup milk

Four tablespoons fat

Mix together well,

Grease pan

Pour mixture into this and pat down with spoon.

Bake at about 425 degrees only about 15 minutes.

* * * *

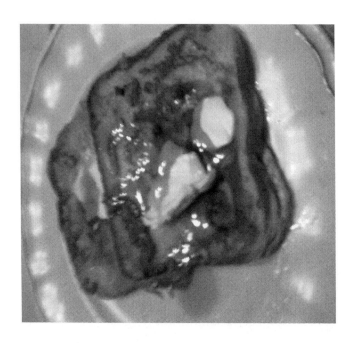

Chapter 3: When it's time for Dessert

Cup cakes with banana

Two large bananas
Two cups self rising flour
Two-thirds cup cooking oil
One cup of sugar
Teaspoon of vanilla or orange juice
Two eggs
One half cup milk

Mash bananas.
Mix flour, shortening, sugar, flavor and eggs in bowl.
Mix well, then add banana and milk and when mixed fill into greased and floured cup cake pans about half full. Add touch of cinnamon on top.
Bake. When cool serve with whipped cream or ice cream

WHEN IT IS TIME FOR SOMETHING SWEET

Lady Fingers

Three egg whites,
One-third cup self rising flour,
One-third cup powered sugar
Two egg yolks,
One-fourth teaspoon vanilla.

Add one eighth teaspoon salt to egg whites and beat until stiff and dry. Fold in sugar slowly. Then add the yolks, beaten until thick. Add flavoring. Mix flour into this. Drop by spoonfuls onto pan. Bake 350 degrees about 10 minutes.

Hint: A good cook starts with a willing pair of hands and the desire to try, try again.

* * *

GREEN APPLE PIE

Six green apples, peeled and cut in large pieces
One cup sugar
One teaspoon cinnamon
Two tablespoons water

Put unbaked pie crust in pie pan. Add sliced apples, sprinkle with sugar, and slices of butter (about half a stick), the cinnamon, the water. Put the slices of margarine here and there on the mixture before putting top crust on.
Place the top crust on and punch holes about four in the center with fork.

Bake 45 minutes at 425 degrees.

* * *

Pie Crust with Lard

All crusts should be baked until they shake freely from pan.

Three cups flour, one teaspoon salt, and two-thirds cup lard, and one-half cup cold water.

Place flour in mixing bow, mix in salt, and mix with fork the lard. Then add water until the mixture holds together in the bowl nicely,

This is enough for one pie, top and bottom.

Bake with pie mixture of choice. (See Apple Pie Recipe above)

* * *

STRAWBERRY PHILADELPHIA CREAM

One cup heavy cream
One cup strawberries

Mash the strawberries thoroughly and sweeten. Put cream in the freezer and when partially frozen, add strawberries. That's it!

* * *

CUSTARD PIE

Two cups milk, hot
Three whole eggs,
One-half cup sugar
One-fourth teaspoon salt
One-fourth teaspoon nutmeg
One-half teaspoon vanilla

Bake well pricked pie shell 10 minutes at 450 degrees. Add three cups of the warm custard mixture to hot shell. Bake five minutes longer at 450 degrees. Turn off flame and let pie continue to cook for ten minutes more. Cool.

* * *

BANANA DELIGHT

Mash and beat three ripe bananas to a cream. Beat whites of three eggs stiff. Fold in banana pulp. Serve in six portions topped with a small spoonful of whipped cream, a cherry and two mint leaves.

* * *

BAKED APPLES

Seven small green apples
Half cup sugar
One and one-half teaspoons cinnamon, half that nutmeg
Three teaspoons flour
Three teaspoons butter
One-half cup water

Wash and core apples. Cut a strip around the middle and place in a baking dish. Mix the sugar, cinnamon and flour and pour into the hold in the middle of the apple. Put butter n each and pour the water in the bottom of the baking dish.
Bake at 400 degrees for 35 to 40 minutes.

* * *

MOLASSES COOKIES

One cup shortening
One cup molasses
One cup brown sugar
One-half cup milk
Three cups flour
Two teaspoons soda, one teaspoon salt and two teaspoons vanilla

Bake this at 375 degrees for about 10 minutes.

* * *

CUSTARD SAUCE

One and one-half cups milk
One-fourth cup sugar
Two eggs
One-eighth teaspoon salt
One-half teaspoon vanilla.

Heat the milk on low heat. Mix the sugar with the eggs which have been beaten. Add this slowly to the scalded milk, stir constantly until thickened. Remove from fire and add the salt and vanilla and then chill.

* * *

APPLE CANDY CAKE

This is a cake and a candy, two in one treat!
Two cups canned apple sauce
One-half cup brown sugar
Two tablespoons butter
Two tablespoons lemon juice
One teaspoon cinnamon
One-half teaspoon allspice
One-fourth teaspoon salt
Three cups self-rising flour with one-third cup shortening mixed together.
Two cups cream
One-half cup sugar
One teaspoon vanilla
One-fourth teaspoon nutmeg

Combine apple sauce, brown sugar, butter, ginger, lemon juice, cinnamon, allspice and salt in pan. Simmer over low heat, stir. Until thick and smooth. Cool.

Take your pastry mix into bowl (The flour and shortening mix) and Blend in three-fourths cup apple sauce. Divide into four parts. And roll each part into an 8 inch square. Place squares on baking sheets and press over bottoms of inverted eight inch baking pans. Bake at 425 degrees until layers are firm. Cool and then lift layers from pans with spatula. Whip cream until stiff. Fold in remaining apple sauce mixture, sugar, vanilla and nutmeg. Spread between and over top of layers. Chill for eight hours.

* * *

CUP CAKES

One-half cup margarine
One cup sugar
Two eggs
Two-thirds cup milk,
One and three-fourths cups of flour
One and one-half teaspoons baking powder
 One-fourth teaspoon salt
One teaspoon vanilla

Cream the margarine and sugar together. Stir in beaten eggs; add milk alternating with the flour. When this is smooth, add vanilla. Bake at 375 degrees for about 20 minutes.

* * *

Chapter 4: Main stay of the meal: Vegetables

SWEET POTATOES WITH APPLES

Four sweet potatoes
Three cooking apples (prefer green skins)
One-fourth cup brown sugar light
Five tablespoons margarine
Cup of water
Trim skin of sweet potatoes and then slice thin. Do the same on apples. Mix these in pan.

Mix other items in small saucepan on low heat until mixed well. Pour the spice mixture over the potato and apple mixture and cook on low heat, covered until soft. Add water if necessary.

* * *

LET'S COOK SOME BEANS

Start with any slow cooker crock pot
Package Pinto beans or navy beans
One onion
Water two-third full
Cook all night.
I always wash beans first, some people don't, but I wash everything I cook, and I mean everything.
I have to watch the salt, so I don't salt this.
This is a favorite in our family and I fix it different variations, its according to who has really wanting me to cook the beans.
Sometimes I add chili mix and tomatoes, for chili beans.
Sometimes I add pork neck bones.

When this is done, I put in bigger pot, add cooked chili meat and we have chili.

* * *

I have cooked the beans in a pot and people add this to their chili if they want beans and I made the chili without beans.

* * *

Don't get in a hurry cooking beans; it takes as long as it takes. I have found some of the older recipes do take a while, but they are still just as good as they were when they were cooked during the old Western Days and during The Great Depression!

* * *

Hint: Serve the cornbread with this. Recipe in this book!

* * *

STUFFED GREEN PEPPERS

Eight large green peppers

Two pounds beef
One large onion
One and one-half cups rice
Two tomatoes

Cut tops of peppers and clean out seeds and stem. Take the tops and trim middle out and take what's left and fry in a little grease, add meat and two tablespoons milk and cook for five or ten minutes. Add tomatoes and rice.

Boil the peppers in salted water fifteen minutes. Drain and fill with the mixture, sprinkled with bread crumbs and butter and put in oven to brown.

* * *

POTATO PANCAKES

One cup flour
Two teaspoons salt
Two teaspoons baking powder
Two eggs, unbeaten
One cup milk
Four tablespoons of butter or margarine
Two tablespoons grated onion
Two cups mashed potatoes

Mix this together. Drop by tablespoons onto pan with cooking oil in it. Fry and then turn over and fry (like pancakes)

* * *

CABBAGE

Cooked: Take one head of cabbage, wash and remove the outer leaves just one layer only. Cut cabbage in half and then slice into slices and when done put this in your deep pan. I add about a quart of water and salt to taste. Boil this until cabbage is tender. Some add some type of fat to this, such as a neck bone or two.

* * *

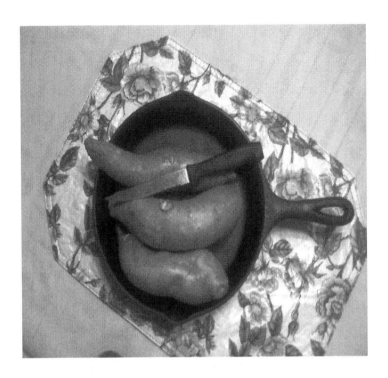

SWEET POTATOES

I like to bake sweet potatoes in the oven when I am baking a chicken or something like that. It only takes a few minutes to bake the sweet potato, and you can serve this in the skin. Split it open and add butter while it is hot!

* * *

BAKED BEANS

Take Great Northern Beans and cook in crock-pot with water all night.

Take bacon about six slices and chop, one green pepper, one onion, can tomato juice (large), and a tablespoon prepared mustard.

Cook all of this in crock pot until beans are tender. Can reheat by putting in oven or microwave to heat and eat. Sometimes I fry frankfurters and slice and put this on top of finished dish.

A warm meal.

* * *

ASPARAGUS

Two pounds asparagus
Boiling water
One teaspoon salt

Wash thoroughly and remove the tough ends from the asparagus. Add boiling water to cover and the salt. Boil for about 20 minutes or until tender.

* * *

CORN

When you buy corn, you need to pull a few of the green leaves away to see if it has blackened kernels or rotten kernels, signs of worms or disease.

Fresh corn will have some of this, but you can peel the green skins off and the silken part and then wash the corn well. Sometimes I add a little salt to the wash bad just to be sure I clean it well.

You need to break the hard end off of the ear of corn, or cut it off, and cut off the black or rotten places as you would with potatoes.

When clean, put in deep pan, add water to cover, and may add lid, but leave a way for steam to escape or it will boil over. Cook about thirty minutes.

* * *

Hint: An excellent meal, fresh corn on the cob, sliced ham, fried or baked, and potatoes.

* * *

Chapter 5: Fish and things from the Sea

FOR LESSONS IN COOKING AND LIVING, LOOK BACK AT THE OLD WAYS

FISH A LA KING

White sauce: Make by two tablespoons shortening, melted. Add two tablespoons flour and dash salt and pepper. When mixed, add one cup milk. Cook low heat until thickened. To this add large can drained tuna, dash of paprika, a half cup peas and chopped hard cooked egg.

* * *

TUNA CROQUETTES

Four tablespoons shortening
One-half cup flour
One teaspoon salt
Dash pepper
One cup of milk, one 7 oz. can tuna fish drained
One teaspoon grated onion
One tablespoon lemon juice
Two hard cooked eggs, diced
Fine cracker crumbs
One egg beaten

Melt butter, then add flour, salt and pepper, and then stir well. Gradually add milk and thicken then remove from heat. Add tuna, onion, lemon juice and hard cooked egg, blend well, mix crackers a few at a time, crushed, until the mixture is firm enough to put in patties or balls and fry in shortening until brown.

* * *

SHRIMP

Boil shrimp seven or eight minutes in water with a dash of salt. Drain and shell and clean of veins. Serve with shrimp sauce.

* * *

FRIED FISH

With fish fillets:
One egg, beaten
Two tablespoons water
Cornmeal, salt and pepper
Shortening

Wash fillets and dry. Dip in water and then seasoned corn meal. Melt shortening and cook fillets until brown on both sides.

* * *

PAN FRIED FRESH FISH

Any kind of fish crappie, perch
Shortening
Flour
Salt and pepper

Prepare fish for cooking and fillet. Melt shortening, and coat fish with flour. Fry on both sides until brown and flaking apart.

* * *

FRIED MACKEREL

You can fix a can of mackerel the same way you do any tuna or salmon dish. I prefer to take a can of mackerel, remove bones and skin. Take a whole cracker, crumble into fish, and one egg, a dash of milk, mix with a tablespoon or more of flour until it holds enough to put by spoonfuls into a pan of melted shortening to fry. Fry on both sides.

* * *

TUNA SALAD SANDWICHES

Two large cans of tuna drained
One onion chopped
Two boiled eggs chopped
About three tablespoons mayonnaise
And that is it. Put this on toasted bread for just sliced bread and it is a quick, nutritious sandwich.

* * *

TUNA DINNER

Six cups sliced peeled potatoes
One-fourth cup margarine
One-fourth cup flour
Salt, pepper,
Three and one-half cups milk
One cup grated cheese
One and one-half cup peeled and sliced onion
One-half green pepper diced

One or two large cans of tuna
One-half cup dry break crumbs, toasted and crushed

Place potatoes in pan. Add water and sale and boil until tender. Set aside, and wash and in a dry fry pan mix butter melted, flour, salt and pepper, then milk, stir until thickened. Then cheese, stir until melted. Add tuna and the meal is ready.

* * *

AN OLD ICE CHEST

SPECIAL SALADS TO GO WITH THAT MEAL

BANANA SALAD

Chop two bananas, chop lettuce, and put the banana on the lettuce with a half cup cottage cheese with a cherry topping. Serve with mayonnaise.

* * *

POTATO SALAD

Eight large potatoes. Cook in boiling water in skins until soft and done. Cool. Take two hard boiled eggs, one onion, one cup sour pickles, and one-fourth cup mustard and same of mayonnaise. When potatoes are done, peal and chop. Add the rest of ingredients chopped. Add mustard and mayonnaise last. Mix well and chill. Must keep cold if taken on picnic.

* * *

AMBROSIA

Two cups strawberries
Two cups crushed pineapple
One cup seedless grapes
One cup pear pieces
Two cups fruit juice (Orange))
Half cup peaches
All fruits are chopped
Now soak three tablespoons of gelatin in one-half cup of water and then dissolve this in the hot fruit juice and chill.

Blend with mayonnaise, stir gently into fruits, beat one cup cream, whipped very stiff, and fold into fruit mixture. Pour into freezing trays of refrigerator and freeze three hours.

* * *

MACARONI SALAD

One package macaroni, cooked
Can pimentos
Four slices cheese, diced.
Mayonnaise dressing
Diced celery stalk, slice of diced apple if desired
Two sweet pickles diced.

To macaroni, add pimentos, cheese, and rest and mix well.

* **

EASY CABBAGE SLAW

Take one head of cabbage, clean and take outer leaves off and discard.

Cut this in half and then put wedges into food processor in pieces. Chop fine. Put in bowl and add mayonnaise. Chill and serve.

* * *

BEAN SALAD

Take left over pinto beans or kidney beans, shredded carrot, cabbage, and mayonnaise. I sometimes add raisins. This can be made with two colors of cabbage, and one tomato, and even some chopped lettuce, or a large salad combination. Top with shredded cheese.

* * *

PINEAPPLE SALAD

One pint cream
One cup cream cheese
One-half cup salad dressing
One pound small marshmallows
Large can of crushed pineapple

Beat the cream until real stiff and fold into the mixture. Pack into trays in freezer and freeze three hours. Serve with salad dressing and maraschino cherries on top.

* * * *

Chapter 6: The best of the best, fresh fruits

FRUIT IS ALWAYS A GREAT IDEA

Hint: Make it a serious part of each month's budget to seek out fresh fruit sales. It is a good way to start a grocery list.

* * *

Suggestions:
Apples
Pineapples
Plums
Apricots
Blackberries
Cherries,
Peaches
Pears

Watermelon
Cantaloupe
Strawberries

* * *

KEEPING HOUSE WISELY

It is the little things which make a household manage well and lead to both health and happiness. It is the attention to detail when spending money during times of economizing which help keep this beautiful harmony of the people who live in the house.

Wastefulness on the grocery list, splurging for something not needed, and not really worth the price which it costs can lead to a month of heart ache. Best to agree to save money on the grocery bill, but also to see that the quality of food does not suffer in the process!

* * *

CHOW MEIN

One pound pork, one beef, and one of veal, all diced
Fat one-half cup
Water two cups
Onions two cups
Celery sliced six cups
Salt and pepper
Cornstarch one-fourth cup
Water one cup
Soy sauce one-half cup
Bean sprouts, five cups
Mushrooms one cup
Water chestnuts sliced enough in cans to serve eight

Brown meat in fat. Add water onions, celery, salt and pepper, cover and cook about 10 minutes, and then add cornstarch mixed with water, and then add soy sauce, bean sprouts, mushrooms and chestnuts. Cool and stir until thickened. Serve on hot rice.

* * *

FAMILY SPAGHETTI ITALIAN

Package of spaghetti
Two pounds hamburger
One large can tomato juice
One-fourth cup chili powder
Diced onion, one
Garlic, dash
Fix spaghetti according to directions. Cook hamburger until it changes color, and drain.

Combine the tomato juice, and chili powder, onion and garlic and bring to a boil for about ten minutes.

Serve the spaghetti on a plate, top with meat, and then the tomato mixture, or mix all of these in a large pan and serve already mixed.

* * *

MEXICAN CORN DISH

Hamburger two pounds or three
Onion, green pepper, one each, chopped
Can whole kernel corn
Tomato juice large can
Chili powder three tablespoons
Cumin (if you have it) two teaspoons.
Cook meat and drain. Add rest of ingredients adding the chili powder and cumin first, then onion, green pepper, corn and finally tomato juice.

Can add macaroni to this if you want.
* * *

Serve with cornbread

* * *

This miniature rolling pin and the other kitchen tool reflect things used in the kitchens for many years even dating back to The Great Depression and beyond. Making bread and biscuits is a good way to pinch pennies in the kitchen.

* * *

BASIC COOKING

Bacon can be cooked by putting in a skillet without grease and cook on medium heat. Turn over a few times. When cooked and brown, take up.

Sausage comes in various types. Mainly to cook a sausage patty, cook as you would bacon, but many sausage meats are very lean, so in order not to stick in the pan, I put a little cooking oil in skillet or pan. Mash out the patties by hand and turn over when done.

For sausage links, sometimes these are all right not to add any fat to the skillet, but cook low enough to thoroughly cook inside and out.

* * *

HAMBURGER

The cheaper cuts you buy, normally the more grease the frying meat makes. Sometimes, you can pour this off while frying, but be careful, it is very hot.

You can mash out patties by hand, and put in skillet without any grease if regular hamburger. Cook until brown, turning once or twice. Let it firm up on one side, before turning, or it will fall apart.

Some people like to add bread crumbs and things like that, but I save this for meat loafs and meat balls.

* * *

FRIED OKRA

Wash and cut tops off. Then slice into small slices. Drop into bowl of flour or cornmeal, and shake off excess before dropping okra into heated cooking oil. I drop one in and if it starts sizzling and browning along the side, I put more.

ONION RINGS

Onion rings can be cooked this simple way, but you need to mix them in beaten egg before you flour them. These do better if you use self-rising flour which makes the crust puffier!

* * *

YELLOW SQUASH

Wash and slice, take off stem. Do these the same way as above.

* * *

* * * *

Chapter 7: Care to cook a very cheap meal

Here is a list:

1. Frankfurters with canned chili sauce
2. Cold chicken sandwich
3. Grilled cheese sandwiches
4. Egg omelets

FRANKFURTER MEAL

Frankfurters can be fried lightly in a skillet until brown. It doesn't take any grease basically, but you can add cooking oil to the skillet if you like the frankfurters to have that outdoor seared finish.

Chili sauce is usually much cheaper than cans of chili.

Serve the hot dogs plain or with relish and mustard or mayonnaise. These are good on buns or just sliced bread.

COLD CHICKEN SANDWICH

Remove bones of any leftover chicken and chop, even in a processor if you want it to have the texture of tuna fish. Add chopped onion, and mayonnaise, and then serve on bread. Add sliced tomato and piece of lettuce if desired.

GRILLED CHEESE SANDWICH

Get your ingredients ready and then heat skillet. Take two pieces of bread and butter both sides of them. Place these in skillet and brown lightly on one side. Add a slice of American cheese to one of these pieces of bread in the pan, and top it with the browned other slice. You now have a sandwich in the pan and you carefully brown the top and bottom of this sandwich. Cheese should melt as you brown these.

EGG OMELET

People cook omelets with a great deal of artistic flare. As for me, I start with four eggs, and a dash of milk. In a side dish I put the things I want to put into my omelet. This varies just cheese, chopped meat, or peppers and tomatoes. I start the skillet with a thin layer of cooking oil and pour the beat eggs into the pan. As it spreads out into the hot pan, I take a spatula and shove the run off back towards the center of the pan. As I do this, the runny part will spill out to the sides. This is done quickly. Soon there is a firm egg, resembling a pancake in the pan, and I scrape this to get any really raw egg out to the edges so it will cook. Unfortunately, all of this has to be done fast and with practice. Then I add my bowl of filling into it, again, sometimes just cheese, or a simple cheese omelet, and then fold the mixture in the pan in half. Cook on that side, and some turn this carefully over if they feel it is not quite done. Then lift the finished omelet out of the pan. I serve this cut into sections to several hungry people.

* * * *

MACARONI WITH TOMATO JUICE AND SPICES, AND FRIED POTATOES

MACARONI WITH CHEESE

Small bag macaroni or half large bag
One cup grated cheese,

Cook macaroni
Drain macaroni

Immediately add cheese and two cups of milk.

Stir well. If you have to heat slightly to melt cheese, do so.

* * *

CHILI MAC

Cook macaroni and drain. Cook two pounds of hamburger with chopped onion, and drain of grease. Mix these together with three tablespoons chili powder, dash of garlic, and large can of stewed tomatoes.

MACARONI SALAD

Cooked macaroni drained and cool
One chopped pepper,
Two hard boiled eggs chopped
Add mayonnaise about one cup and mix.

You may add things to this last recipe such as a can of drained pinto beans, and some shredded cheddar cheese.

SPAGHETTI IS EASY TO MAKE

Take a package of spaghetti and put into boiling water. Soften and cook about 15 minutes. Drain.

For the meat, brown hamburger, and drain.

For the sauce, either a can of spaghetti sauce, or use the small cans of tomato sauce, with about one tablespoon of chili powder added to the meat before you add the sauce. Heat this together and mix and serve.

* * *

**SOME PEOPLE LIKE TO GRIND THEIR OWN
COFFEE, AND FALL BACK ON THE OLD WAYS**

* * * *

Chapter 8: Basic lessons about Meat

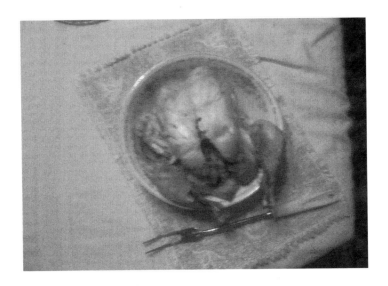

Hint: I sometimes cook one meal, freeze parts of it for later. When I roast a chicken, I do that, and when I want to make a chicken and noodle casserole or something like that, it is easy to get cooked chicken out of the freezer and use that. It helps when I am having a very busy day, too busy to cook. The featured whole chicken was roasted in an electric roaster, just with water.

BARBECUE CHICKEN

Large chicken
Flour
Cup of shortening
One large onion, sliced
One clove garlic, finely minced
One teaspoon prepared mustard
Three tablespoons steak sauce
Two tablespoons brown sugar
Three cups tomato juice

Cut chicken into serving pieces and shake flour over this. Melt shortening and fry chicken until brown and done. I would cover this while frying and check and turn often. Combine garlic, onion, prepared mustard. Then mix steak sauce, brown sugar and tomato juice and pour over chicken. Cook until tender.

FRANKFURTERS AND SAUERKRAUT

Take one package frankfurters and boil until plump.
Open two cans sauerkraut and heat.

Simple meal served with peas or beans and cornbread

* * *

MEAT LOAF

Four pounds hamburger
Crackers (two large crumbled)
Day old bread crumbled about four
Two eggs
Tomato juice one cup
Combine this, add cup of milk.

Make into a meat roll in oven pan. Top with a can of tomato
sauce or some catsup.

Bake uncovered and when done pour off grease before serving

I sometimes add chopped green pepper and onion when I have
them.

* * *

ROAST HAM

Always wash a ham and then you can roast it in a roaster with
about three quarts of water. The roaster is covered, and cook the ham
for one hour or slightly longer, (425 or thereabouts) then turn heat
off and let it continue to cook until the roaster is cooled off. I then
slice the meat into various servings for different meals and freeze in
a container until use.

To roast ham in an oven, wash ham, place in deep oven pan and you can sprinkle with a little brown sugar, and stick cloves in the skin of ham. Cover with aluminum foil and cook at a low heat, about 325 for a couple of hours. Check this oven temperatures vary.

I serve the ham with green beans, baked potatoes, and a salad and fruit dessert.

* * *

PORK ROAST

Start with nice pork roast and roasting pan for stove. I wash the roast, then put it in the pan and add a little cooking oil and brown roast slightly in low heat. This is called searing by some people also. Then I add water and cover the roast. Obviously this takes a deep pan. I cook on a medium temperature for hours until tender. This is with a lid and check from time to time. If the water gets very low, I add some, but don't add cold water. Run the water in the tap until hot, and add hot water to the cooking roast.

I like to serve this with sweet potatoes which can be peeled and boiled also. I sometimes add the potatoes to the roast when the roast is about done and cook for about 20 minutes or less.

* * *

FRIED SWEET POTATOES

For variety, cut cold cooked sweet potatoes into thick slices. Dip these into egg beaten with a dash of milk. Then stir the potatoes up in a bowl of crushed cornflakes, or flour. Fry until brown and put on paper to drain.

* * *

SPARERIBS

Ten pounds of spareribs
Four small cans tomato sauce

Two tablespoons chili powder
One tablespoon steak sauce
Two chopped onions
One green pepper chopped

Take the spareribs and bake covered in oven until tender. Bake them with one cup of water.

Then mix your barbecue mix and pour this over spare ribs and cook thirty minutes more.

* * *

One of my favorite things to make is chili and there are so many varieties and styles of this now. Start with a chili mix from the store, or an easy recipe and go from there, experience and have fun developing your own family recipe.

* * * *

Chapter 9: Rich dishes seem simple, but they aren't

CUCUMBER ICE

Four cucumbers
One stalk celery
One green pepper
One large onion
Bowl of mayonnaise

Cut cucumbers into long halves, scrape out inside into a pulp. Get out seeds you can. Chop celery, pepper and onion very well. Add mayonnaise. Freeze mixture about three hours.

* * *

CREAM POTATOES

Take eight potatoes, peel and dice. Put in pan and cover with water and boil until they fall apart when pierced with a fork. Drain water off of these. Do not undercook, lumpy potatoes are the result. Now add one half cup milk, one third stick butter and mash with fork, mixer, or hand held potato masher.

This recipe seems very simple, yet people try to undercook the potatoes and these can really stay too hard to eat. The next problem is watery potatoes, drain completely. But if you follow the simple directions, and follow them exactly, they will be a good dish.

* * *

EGGS

An egg is a simple thing to cook but can be ruined in countless ways. Preparation is important. For one egg, a small iron skillet is worth the investment. People have been cooking in iron skillets for hundreds of years, even before they were cooking using stoves. I myself have cooked cornbread while camping out using my old iron skillet and then would take it back home and cook eggs in it on the stove. They are that versatile. Some of the older ones are extremely heavy; I think one of the heaviest I ever had was an old fashioned Dutch oven, a deep dish skillet, very large with its own lid. This was a massive thing to carry around for any reason, but could you cook in it. The answer is yes!

Some of the older ones are around in second hand stores and things like that. Newer ones are available many places. The older ones, when we wanted to really clean them, we would take them out, build a fire and burn them clean. Newer ones I wouldn't try this, in fact it just isn't done anymore.

I believe stainless steel pans are very serviceable and last. My mother gave me a stainless steel pan many years ago and it is as fresh and useable as it was well over 20 years ago.

It pays, when thinking about thrifty ways to save money in the kitchen, I believe it is like a business in its own way, and a lot of thought should be taken on the tools which will be used there.

* * *

PARKER HOUSE ROLLS

For as long as I can remember, the baking of bread has been a wonder and a necessity in most cultures. Rolls can make any meal better.

One cup milk
One cake compressed yeast
Four tablespoons sugar
Four tablespoons fat
Four cups flour
One and one-half teaspoon salt
One egg

Fix yeast in bowl with sugar and one-fourth cup lukewarm water. Add sugar to this.

Mix by adding the beaten egg after half of the flour has been added. Alternate flour with milk. Add fat. Mix in. Put on a board or table and knead well, punch down and pick up, wad it up, then punch with knuckles down. Add flour to the bread if it sticks. When you have done this about fifteen minutes, put in pan or bowl to rise. Cover with tower. When it has risen to double in bulk smooth the dough on a floured board until it is about one-half inch thick.

Cut with a small biscuit cutter into rounds. Let stand a few minutes, and then crease with the dull side of a knife just a little at one side of the middle.

Brush the smaller side with melted butter and fold over the wider side.

Place far enough apart to prevent them from touching one another. Let rise until double in bulk. Bake at 400 degrees for 15 to 20 minutes.

* * *

Chapter 10: how many kinds of gravy are there?

APRICOT SAUCE

One-half pound dried apricots
One-third cup sugar
Six tablespoons water
One tablespoon lemon juice
Soak apricots and cook slowly until tender. Put through a blender and strainer. Add sugar and water to pulp and cook five minutes. Add lemon juice and serve hot or cold. May add more water to make thinner.

* * *

BROWN GRAVY

One tablespoon butter
One tablespoon flour
One cup beef stock
Salt and pepper

Brown butter in saucepan, add flour and brown. Add liquid and stir until smooth and thick. Season to taste.

* * *

PACCALLILI

Two quarts green tomatoes
Two heads celery
Four red peppers

Two green peppers
Four large cucumbers
Two large white onions
One cup salt
One and one-half quarts vinegar
Two pounds light brown sugar
One-fourth cup white mustard seed
One teaspoon mustard
One and one-half teaspoons black pepper

Chop vegetables in chopper, sprinkle with salt, and let stand over night and drain in morning. Drain thoroughly. Add vinegar sugar and spices and simmer until vegetables are tender and clear.

* * *

Hint: Even if you don't do home canning, buy one dozen quart jars, wide mouth with lids and use to store things in ice box, from fruit juices, powdered milk mixed for use, and things like this relish!

* * *

FRENCH DRESSING

One-teaspoon onion juice
One-fourth teaspoon pepper
Three-fourths teaspoon salt
One teaspoon paprika
Three-fourth cup olive oil
Two tablespoons vinegar
Two tablespoons lemon juice.

Mix the seasonings together and add the oil. Beat and then pour the vinegar and lemon juice slowly on these ingredients, beating until the dressing is thickened.

* * *

HOLLANDAISE SAUCE

One-half cup butter

Four egg yolks, well beaten
One-half cup boiling water
Dash of cayenne pepper
One-half teaspoon salt
One and one-half tablespoons lemon juice

In good sauce pan melt butter and slowly add egg yolks, sir constantly. Gradually add water. Continue stirring and cook until mixture begins to thicken. Slow down, even turn off and add pepper, sale and lemon juice, stir well. Don't over cook or it will separate.

* * *

REMEMBER, SIMPLE AND HEALTHY!

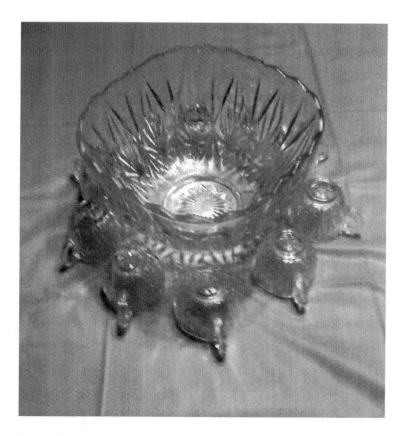

PUNCH: Make syrup by boiling one and one-half cups sugar and four cups water twenty minutes. Add cider, orange juice and lemon juice. Cool, strain and pour into pitcher to cook in refrigerator freezer until mushy.

* * * *

Chapter 11: What is a meal without bread?

SHORT BISCUIT

Six cups flour
One teaspoon salt
Three teaspoons cream of tartar
One and one-half teaspoons soda
Two tablespoons butter
Enough milk to make soft dough.

Mix all of the dry ingredients well. Then take the butter and mix this with the mixture using a fork. Add the liquid and stir and shape a ball like mass of dough. Take this onto a board sprinkled with flour and knead (mash) about five times. Add salt before the last mashing of dough.

Take pinches of this and place on cookie sheet. Bake about 15 minutes at 450 degrees.

* * *

FRIED BOLOGNA SANDWICH

Buy thick sliced bologna. Put a small amount of cooking oil in pan. Take one piece of bologna and put it in the pan, it will start curling up so in order to stop this, slit it in center and do this cross-wise. Then turn over after cooked (a few seconds) and fry on that side.

* * *

DEVILED EGGS

Hard boil eggs by putting them in water from regular tap, cold. Cover eggs in the saucepan with water. Bring to a boil and boil ten minutes. Let cool, or take and pour the water off, add cold water out of tap again, and shake pan, breaking shells and they will turn lose faster and make it easier to peel. Once peeled, cut the eggs in half and put whites on a plate, but yolks in a bowl. To the yolks add tablespoon of mustard, and one of mayonnaise. Also add very fine diced pickle. Mix this with a fork, so you can mash yolk and blend well. Take a spoon and take some of this mixture and put it in the half shell of the boiled white part of the eggs. Do these with a teaspoon until you put some of the mixture in all of the white halves. Then sprinkle with paprika for color.

Chapter 12: Sometimes nothing will do but a good soup!

TOMATO SOUP WITH CREAM

One large can tomatoes, or five large tomatoes, pealed with seeds removed
Cook until these are soft with some water.
Add celery seed, pepper and salt,
In a cup take one tablespoon of flour, one of butter and one cut hot milk and mix .this into your soup. This will thicken it and when it is thickened, well, it's done.

* * *

OLD TIME STEW

Four tablespoons shortening
Three pounds of stew meat (any kind) or bones stripped off boney meat
Five cups of water
One onion
Nutmeg
Six potatoes cut into pieces
Five carrots cut into small pieces

Brown meat in shortening, but don't drain. Add water and spaces and cook until meat is tender and done. Then add potatoes and carrots. Add more water if needed, and cook until they are tender.

Chapter 13: Game plan for saving money and learning to cook better

Hint: Never go to the store hungry, you will waste money and buy things you don't need!

* * *

QUICK SCRAMBLED EGGS

Can be breakfast, supper in sandwiches

Take six eggs
Salt and pepper
Butter, about three tablespoons, melted in skillet

If fire is too hot, will burn butter and scorch eggs. Cook on medium heat until scrambled eggs are done. Serve with toast are on bread with mayonnaise.

WHEN COOKING FOR A PARTY OR A LARGE GROUP OF PEOPLE, KEEP IT SIMPLE, BUT IT CAN STILL BE ELEGANT WHEN SERVED AND DELIGHT THE PEOPLE YOU ARE FEEDING.

* * *

SALMON PATTIES

One can salmon
Salt and pepper
Two squares of crackers, four squares per whole cracker, and so eight small squares

Two eggs,
One-half cup milk

Mix thoroughly and then add two tablespoons flour

Melt shortening in skilled and drop salmon by large spoonfuls into plan. Flatten with a spoon. Cook on one side and then the other until brown.

* * *

RICE PUDDING

Two eggs
Two cups milk
One-half cup raisins
One-half cup sugar
One tablespoon powdered sugar
1/4 teaspoon nutmeg
One and one-fourths cups cooked rice
One-fourth teaspoon salt

Separate eggs; add to the yolk two tablespoons milk. Place balance of milk in low heat pan and then raisins add to the milk and cook about five minutes. Add the rice, cook five minutes longer, and stir
In yolks of eggs, salt, sugar and spice.
Stir well, cook about two or three minutes longer. Remove from fire and pour in pudding dish. Beat eggs whites stiff, add powdered sugar, spread on top of pudding and brown slightly in 300 degree oven.

* * *

Hint:
Want a quick barbecue sauce?
Try one-third cup chopped onion, three tablespoons butter, one cup catsup, one-third cup vinegar, two tablespoons brown sugar, one-half cup water

Two teaspoons prepared mustard
Mix and simmer fifteen minutes.

* * *

CANAPES

These are made from day old bread, which is cut into small pieces and sometimes shaped with cookie cutters. They are toasted to delicate brown in preheated over at about 250 degrees.

They can be topped with all sorts of toppings: sardines, caviar, shrimp, cheese and things like that, meats, boiled eggs, sliced and sometimes these toppings, such as tuna are first mixed with mayonnaise.

* * *

ONION RINGS

One onion, sliced
Two eggs beat with a fork
About a cup of self rising flour. Must be self rising to give onion rings their puff!
Cooking oil to fry these in.

After slicing onion, separate pieces and drop into egg, once covered, then drop into flour and stir around with hands or fork. Then drop into fat by using a spoon with holes in it. Cook onion rings until brown and turn them over if you need to brown other side. I get these out and drain. I like to serve these as a snack in individual bowls with the drain for this being a paper napkin in the bowl, or even paper coffee filters in the bowls.

* * *

OLD FASHIONED CHILI

Three pounds ground meat
One tablespoon oregano
One-fourth cup chili powder
Two teaspoons cumin

One tablespoon garlic
One can tomato juice, large
One-fourth cup floor

Cook meat until changes color. Mix the flour, spices together. Add to meat mixture. Then add tomato juice, and one cup of water.

Cook about fifteen minutes.

For variety:

Can make a Frito pie with chips, one onion, one cup grated American cheese, and sometimes I add pinto beans (one cup)

* **

VEGETABLE SOUP

This is a dish you can learn by trying a basic recipe like this and then add your own ideas to make this a family recipe.

Carrots one can
Green beans one can (can be green peas)
Corn whole kernel one can
Three cups of ground beef cooked
Chili powder one-fourth cup
Can tomato juice, large
Six potatoes pealed and cut into small pieces and boiled soft.
Add cabbage and options if you like, and macaroni.

Start with the cooked potatoes, and ground beef. Add these to a deep pan, and then open cans of vegetables into this. Then add tomato juice and chili powder. Add macaroni last and cook this until done and the meal is ready.

* * *

HINT; YES, VEGETABLES ARE GOOD FOR YOU!

Try an assortment when in season. Beets, sliced, or beets small, whole

Broccolis, remove large outer leaves, cut off tough part of stalk, cut into strips. Always wash thoroughly.

Cabbages, shredded, remove wilted outer leaves. Quarter the cabbage and shred into thin strips

Wedges: use a medium-sized head. Cut into several inch wedges. Remove core.

Cauliflower cut off stem and leaves break into flowerets. Wash

* * * *

FRIED BANANAS

Four bananas
One-fourth cup pineapple juice
One tablespoon lemon juice
One-fourth cup flour
Shortening, about three tablespoons
And peel bananas and brush with pineapple and lemon juice. Roll in flour and then cook in cooking oil. Serve immediately.

* * *

Nightfall comes, the kitchen is clean and the day ends. Hope you enjoyed these recipes and the folk wisdom which was served with it.

* * * *

THE END

#####

* * * * *